Stop CODE!

James Noble • Jon Stuart

Contents

Welcome to Micro World! ..... page 2
The Transporter ..... page 5
Stop CODE! ..... page 15

This page is for an adult to read to you. This page is for an adult to read to you.

Welcome to Micro World!

Macro Marvel invented Micro World – a micro-sized theme park where you have to shrink to get in.

A computer called **CODE** controls Micro World and all the robots inside – MITEs and BITEs.

Macro Marvel
(billionaire inventor)

A MITE

A BITE

Disaster strikes!

CODE goes wrong on opening day.
CODE wants to shrink the world.

Macro Marvel is trapped inside the park …

Enter Team X!

Four micro agents – **Max, Cat, Ant** and **Tiger** – are sent to rescue Macro Marvel and defeat CODE.

Mini Marvel joins Team X.

Mini Marvel
(Macro's daughter)

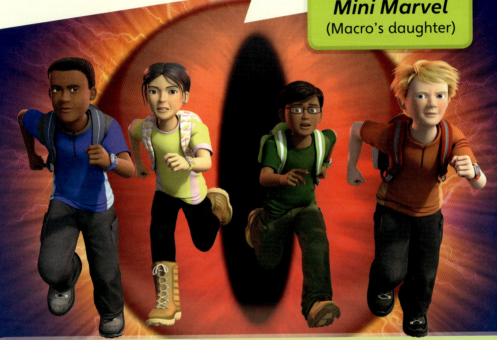

In the last book ...

- Team X got trapped in CODE Control.
- They used their kit to get to the top of CODE.
- Team X put the Master key into CODE but CODE didn't shut down.

**CODE key
(14 collected)**

You are in the CODE Control zone.

This page is for an adult to read with you. This page is for an adult to read with you.

Before you read

Word alert
- Blend the sounds.

  shin**y** uneas**y** desperate**ly** brave**ly**

- Which letter makes the /ee/ sound?

Suffix spotter
- The highlighted letters are suffixes: -y has been added to change the words into describing words (adjectives) and -ly has been added to change the words into words that describe how something was done (adverbs).

What does it mean?

hastily – quickly

Into the zone

- Can you remember how long it will be before CODE shrinks the world?
- How might Team X stop CODE?

The Transporter

Macro Marvel couldn't believe the Master key had failed. Horrified, he covered his head with his hands.

"All is lost," he groaned. "Very soon CODE will shrink the world!"

Desperately, Mini tried to think of a new plan. She noticed the Virus-BITE's CODE key in the desk.

"Dad," said Mini. "Team X only used the first twelve CODE keys to make the Master key. Would it work if we added the CODE keys from the Virus-BITE and the Mega-BITE?"

"Mmm," replied Marvel. "They weren't part of my original design but we could try."

"How will we get the keys to Team X now that CODE has locked the door though?" asked Mini.

"I have an idea ..." said Marvel.

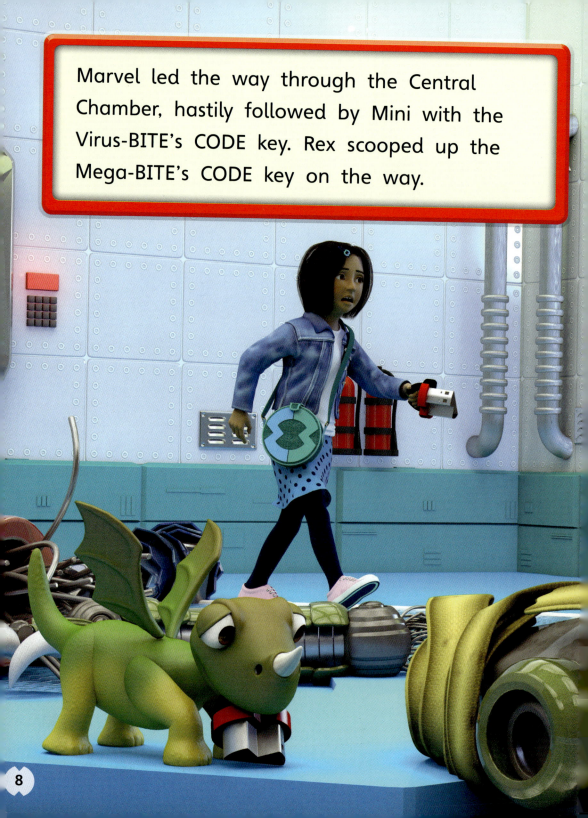

Marvel led the way through the Central Chamber, hastily followed by Mini with the Virus-BITE's CODE key. Rex scooped up the Mega-BITE's CODE key on the way.

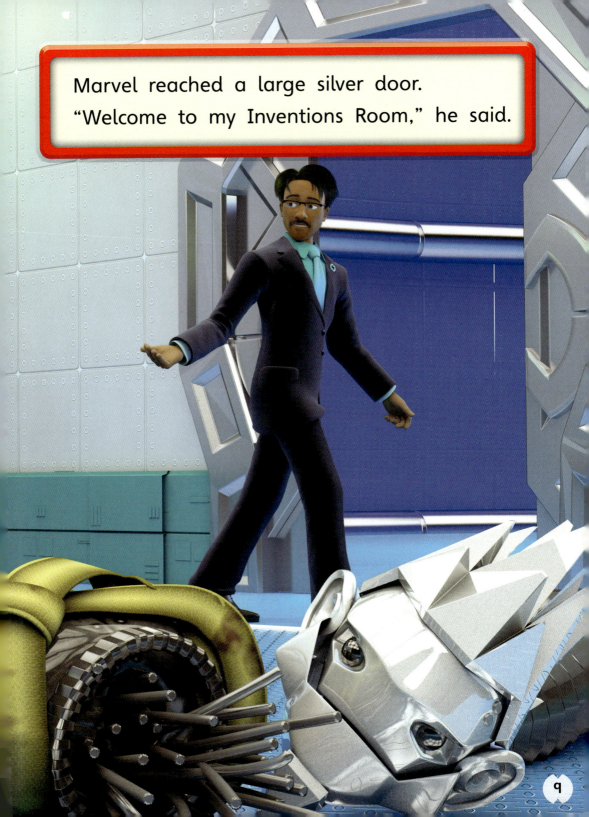

Marvel reached a large silver door. "Welcome to my Inventions Room," he said.

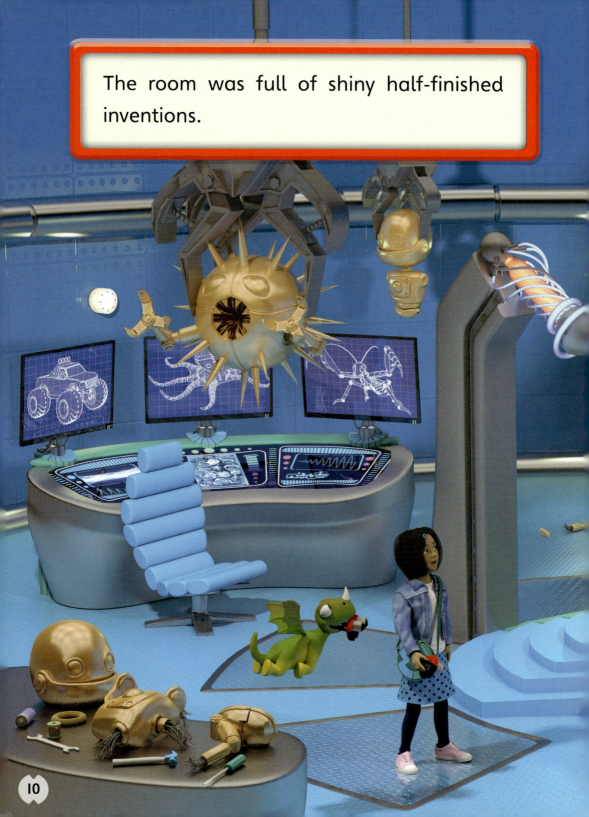

The room was full of shiny half-finished inventions.

"The Transporter is my latest invention," Marvel said. "We can use it to get into CODE Control."

Marvel paused. "I can't set the controls and transport myself at the same time."

"You can transport Rex and me," said Mini.

"It hasn't been tested," sighed Marvel.

"It's the only way we can save Team X and the planet," said Mini, bravely.

Marvel felt uneasy as he pressed the controls.

Now you have read ...
The Transporter

True or false?
Are these sentences true or false?
Use evidence from the story to explain why.

- Mini thinks quickly.   True   False
- Mini isn't very brave.   True   False
- Mini lets her dad do all the work.   True   False

Thinking time
Do you think Mini has changed since she met Team X? Are there any signs that she is braver now?

Say, think, feel
Look at page 12. What did Marvel say about letting Mini use the Transporter? Imagine that you are him. What did he think? How did he feel?

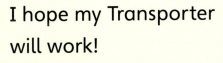

I hope my Transporter will work!

This page is for an adult to read with you.

Before you read

Word alert
- Read the words. Remember the sounds you practised in 'The Transporter'.

  scar**y**   joyful**ly**   proud**ly**

Suffix spotter
- The highlighted letters are suffixes: -y has been added to change the words into describing words (adjectives) and -ly has been added to change the words into words that describe how something was done (adverbs).

What does it mean?

recognisable – something familiar that is easy to identify

Into the zone

- What sort of danger is Team X in?
- What are Mini and Rex taking to Team X?
- Do you think Mini's plan will work?

Stop CODE!
Chapter 1 – Mini to the Rescue

Team X were clinging to each other in terror as CODE rocked the steps below them frantically up and down.
"We need help now!" said Max, desperately hoping for a message on his watch.

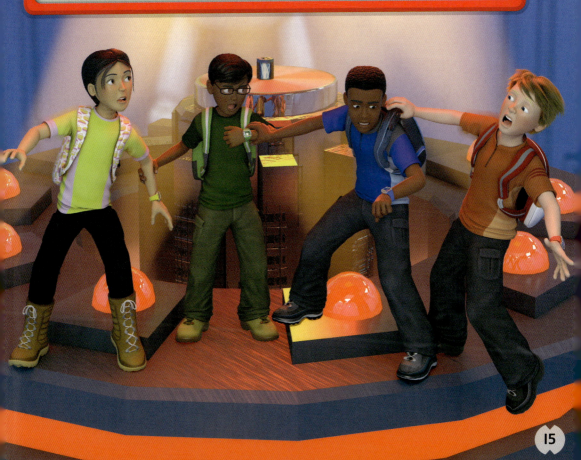

Just then, a small white light appeared, glimmering softly in the corner of CODE Control.

"Look!" Max called to the others.

Little by little, the light grew into two recognisable shapes.

"Mini and Rex!" called Cat joyfully. "How did you manage that trick?"

"I'll explain later," said Mini, holding tightly to the Virus-BITE's CODE key. "Right now, we've got to add these two CODE keys to the Master key."

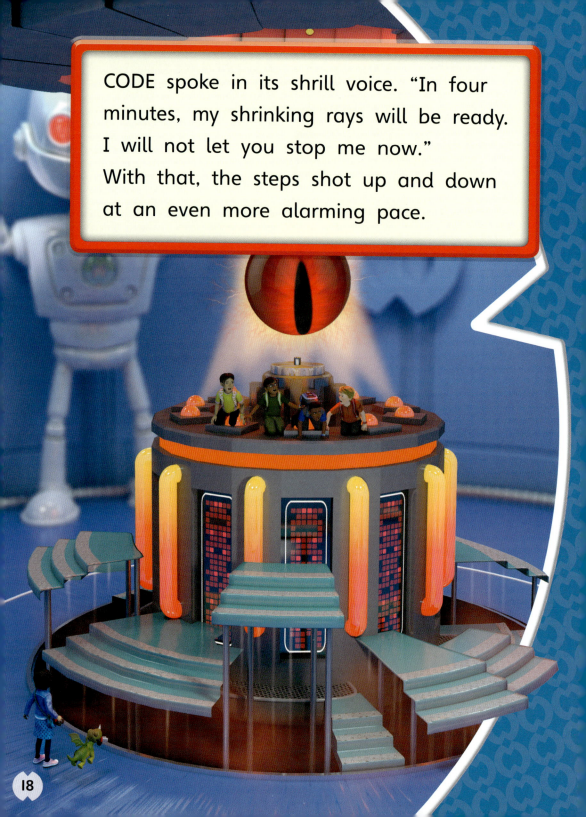

CODE spoke in its shrill voice. "In four minutes, my shrinking rays will be ready. I will not let you stop me now." With that, the steps shot up and down at an even more alarming pace.

Chapter 2 – Countdown

It was almost impossible for Mini to stand on the steps. Every time she tried, the step rocketed up or down, sending her spinning backwards.

"Hold onto this," called Max as he shot out his climbing wire.

With Rex's help, Mini scrambled up.

Team X and Mini crawled towards the Master key.
With a quick tug, Max pulled the key out.
At once, CODE began to vibrate furiously.
"I can't get the extra CODE keys into place," cried Mini.
"One minute to full power!" boomed CODE.

Max and Cat held the Master key steady. At last, Mini slid the final CODE keys into place and the Master key gleamed brightly.
"Please let it work this time," whispered Mini as she moved the key towards the centre of CODE.

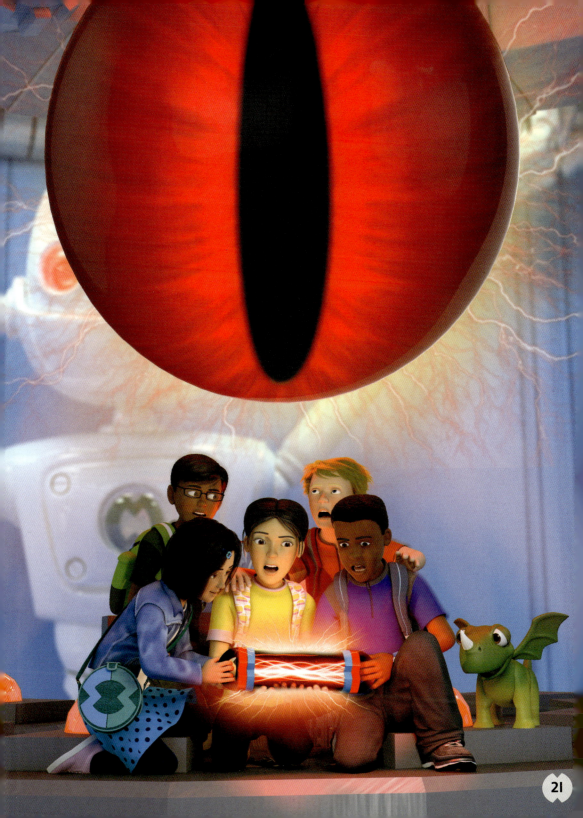

"Aaaargh!" Mini cried out in pain as CODE flashed a bright red light into her eyes.

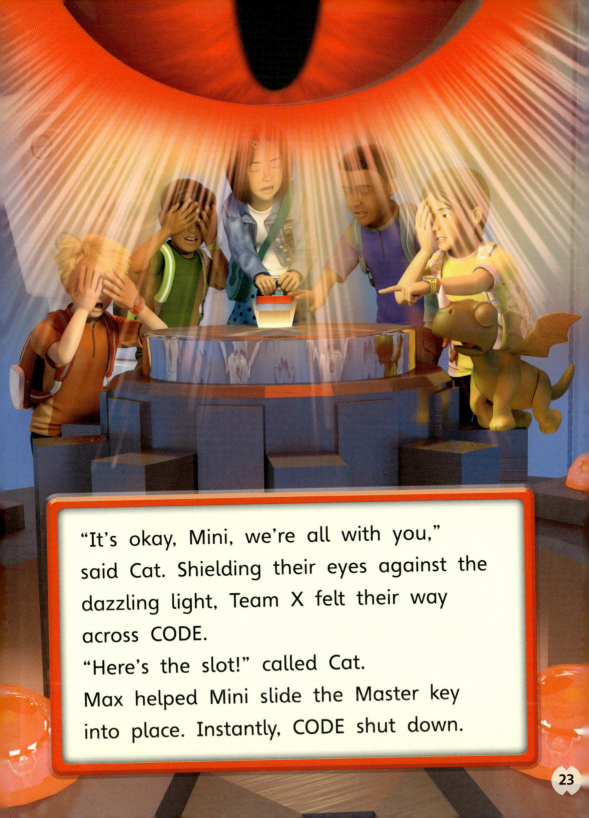

"It's okay, Mini, we're all with you," said Cat. Shielding their eyes against the dazzling light, Team X felt their way across CODE.

"Here's the slot!" called Cat.

Max helped Mini slide the Master key into place. Instantly, CODE shut down.

"It's over!" shouted Mini in relief. "CODE is finished."

Max paused to pull out the Master key. CODE's red eye was trapped inside, glinting horribly.

"Perhaps it isn't over for ever," Max thought. He felt uneasy as he stared at the unblinking eye.

Chapter 3 – Marvel's Reward

Macro Marvel rushed into CODE Control. "You've done it!" he cried. "You've saved the world!"

He hugged Mini. "I'm so glad you're safe. I was so worried!"

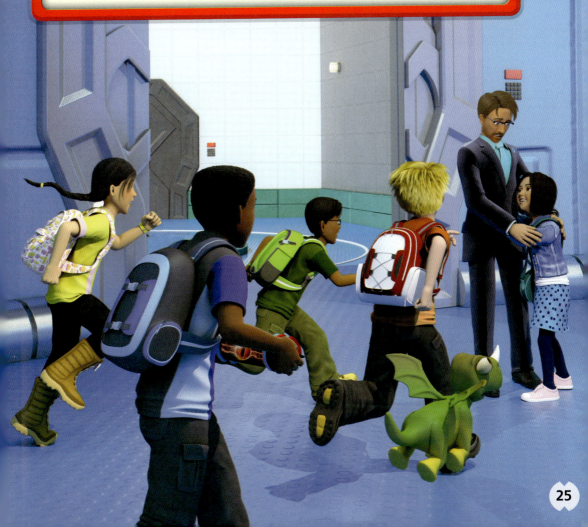

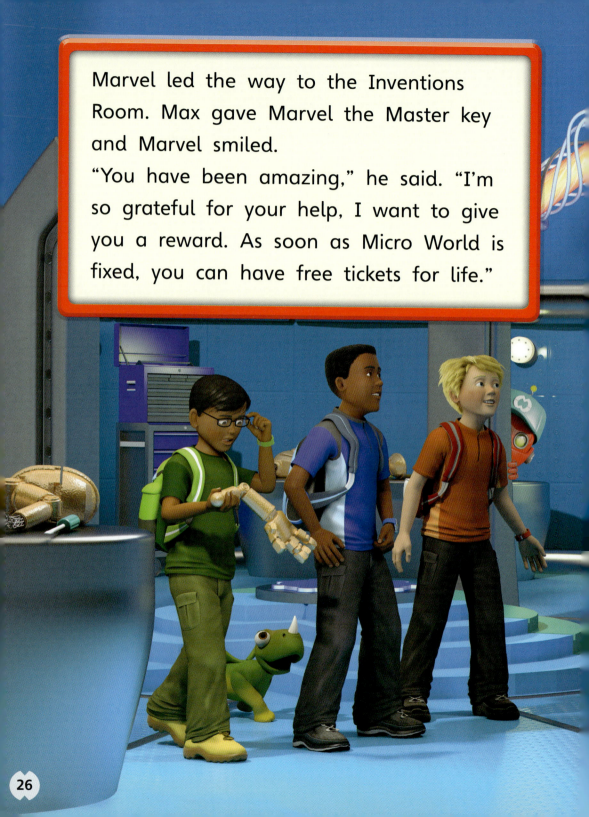

Marvel led the way to the Inventions Room. Max gave Marvel the Master key and Marvel smiled.

"You have been amazing," he said. "I'm so grateful for your help, I want to give you a reward. As soon as Micro World is fixed, you can have free tickets for life."

"Wow! Thank you," said Tiger. Max looked anxious. "How do we know it won't go wrong again?" he asked.

Clutching CODE tightly, Marvel pointed to a big map.

"These lights show where my inventions are," he said proudly. "Each one is powered by a form of CODE and none of them has gone wrong! What happened at Micro World was a strange error. CODE will never go wrong again!"

Team X glanced at each other, uncertainly.

Chapter 4 – Until Next Time …

It was time for Team X to leave Marvel Island. As they wandered back through the park, Tiger looked longingly about him.

A crowd of MITES had gathered on the jetty to wave goodbye.

"Thank you, again," said Mini.

"We'll see you soon," said Tiger. "Next time we meet, we won't be on a dangerous mission, we'll be having fun on the rides!"

Max wasn't so sure. He couldn't get CODE's scary eye out of his mind. As Team X climbed into the Green Dart, Max looked anxious. He hoped Marvel was right that it really *was* the last time they would have to battle CODE.

Now you have read ...
Stop CODE!

Thinking time
On page 29, it says that Tiger looked longingly about him. How do you think he felt about leaving Micro World?
If you went to Micro World, which rides would you like to try?

Shrink the story
Retell the story in just four sentences. Think about the most important event in each chapter.

What next?
Team X and Mini stopped CODE, but is it really all over? Look for clues in the story that suggest CODE might not be defeated.

"Snorp!"

"I'll miss Team X. I hope they come back soon."